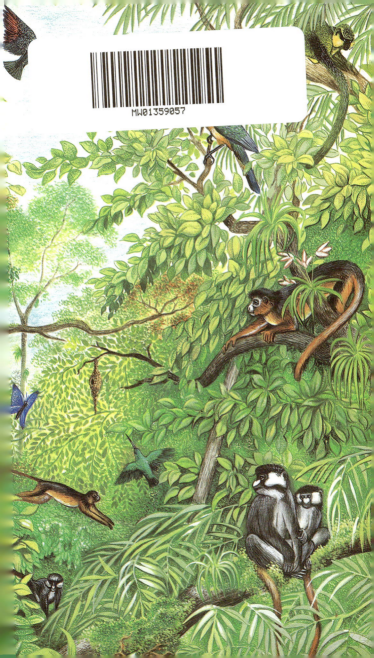

Written by André Lucas
Illustrated by Diz Wallis

Specialist Adviser:
*Patricia Sass, Keeper
Great Apes House
Lincoln Park Zoo*

*ISBN 0-944589-26-X
First U.S. Publication 1989 by
Young Discovery Library
217 Main St. • Ossining, NY 10562*

*©Editions Gallimard 1985
Translated by Vicki Bogard
English text © Young Discovery Library*

YOUNG DISCOVERY LIBRARY

Monkeys, Apes and Other Primates

YOUNG DISCOVERY LIBRARY

"Stop monkeying around!"
say your parents when you
are being silly...
When apes scream, jump up and down,
make their teeth chatter or clap
their hands, they're not fooling
around. That's how they talk!

This **chimpanzee** puts his arm
on top of his head because he's
afraid. Another one crouches
and holds out his hand to make up.

The one looking in his neighbor's fur won't find fleas: apes don't have any! By grooming his friend, he is showing his affection.
There are more than 200 species (kinds) of monkeys, apes and lemurs. Turn the page to see some of them.

Chimpanzees make faces to express all their feelings.

These two chimps hug and thump each other to show their friendship.

Look at your hand: your thumb is opposite the other fingers. It helps you hold objects. Monkeys have feet like hands. That's why they're so good at climbing trees.

A gorilla's foot

A gorilla's hand

The horse's hoof is for running.

The bear's claws are for catching prey.

Did you know that people and apes, monkeys and lemurs, are all members of the **primate** family? Primates have hands good for holding things. Their eyes see colors and can judge both depth and distance.

The mandrill's face looks like a Chinese mask, and so does his behind. That is how the members of the same species can recognize each other.

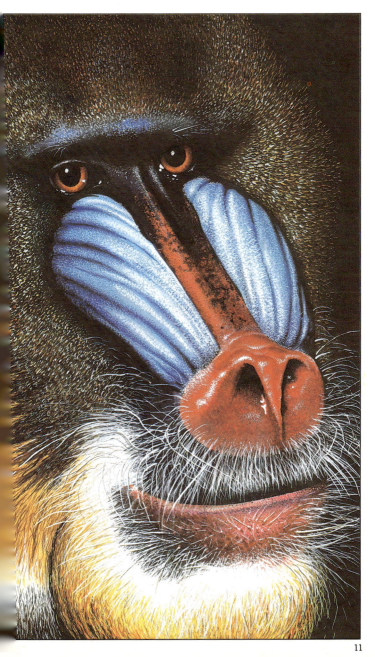

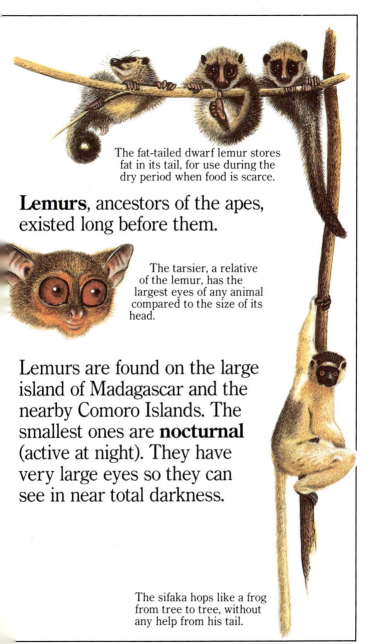

The fat-tailed dwarf lemur stores fat in its tail, for use during the dry period when food is scarce.

Lemurs, ancestors of the apes, existed long before them.

The tarsier, a relative of the lemur, has the largest eyes of any animal compared to the size of its head.

Lemurs are found on the large island of Madagascar and the nearby Comoro Islands. The smallest ones are **nocturnal** (active at night). They have very large eyes so they can see in near total darkness.

The sifaka hops like a frog from tree to tree, without any help from his tail.

Here are the great apes. They are the most like us. The word orang-utang means "old man of the forest" in Malay. Look at these acrobats in the Indonesian forest!

The gibbon lives in the forests of Asia.

The most clever is the chimpanzee. How does he get water from a hollow tree? He uses a handful of chewed leaves to soak up the water like a sponge, then squeezes it into his mouth!

The chimpanzee lives in Africa.

The biggest and strongest is the gorilla! He weighs as much as three men. He's a gentle giant, but it's best not to look him right in the eye. That is a challenge to him!

The gorilla lives in the forests and mountains of Africa.

The hot, wet, dense tropical forest is home to monkeys. They travel in big, noisy groups.
These **squirrel monkeys** are so quick and agile that they can disappear into the branches like magic. Like all South American monkeys, they spend their time in the trees. They use their long tails to keep their balance.

The world's smallest monkey is the pygmy marmoset. One would fit in your pocket! They use their finely-shaped claws to climb trees like squirrels The **woolly monkey** is as gentle as his fur is soft. He is often tamed by the Indians of South America. The **uakari** is nearly bald. The **Diana monkey** is quick and lively. The **De Brazza's monkey** is easy-going. The **drill**, like all baboons, has cheek pockets under his black mask: that's where he keeps extra food.

In Asia, the mother macaque teaches her baby everything. She is very patient.

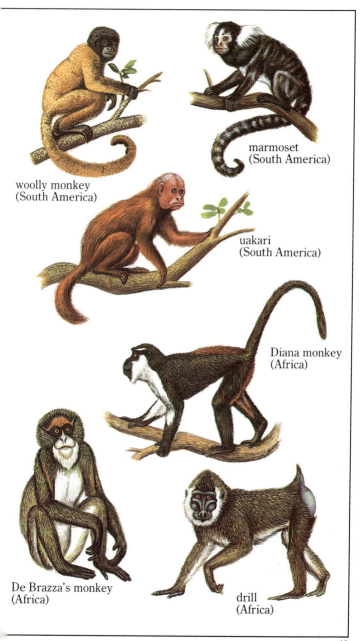

siamang
(Malaysia)

uakari
(Amazon jungle)

proboscis monkey
(Borneo)

snub-nosed or golden monkey
(mountains of China and Tibet)

golden or lion-headed marmoset
(South America)

douroucouli
(South America)

The aye-aye is a lemur. He gnaws a hole in the bark of a tree, then uses his long middle finger to scoop out larvae.

Funny faces!

The **siamang** inflates a sac under its throat like a balloon and howls in the forest. The **uakari**'s face becomes bright red when he gets excited. The **proboscis monkey**'s nose is so big that it hangs in front of his mouth. It gets in his way when he eats!
The **snub-nosed monkey** doesn't have that problem! His heavy fur protects him from the snow.
The **golden marmoset** with his beautiful mane is very rare.

Which is the only nocturnal monkey? The **douroucouli**, with his enormous eyes!

The gibbon flies...

...through the air...
(90 feet above
the ground!)

How do monkeys travel?
Like acrobats! The smaller ones hop from tree to tree on all fours. Some use their tails like an extra arm.

Gorillas move swiftly on ground. Adult males are too heavy to climb trees but females and youngsters do.

What is that…
way high up?
It's a gibbon, prince
of acrobats! With
arms longer than his legs,
he swings from branch to branch
as if he were flying. But
sometimes, he falls…

…with the greatest of ease!
(25 feet in a single bound!)

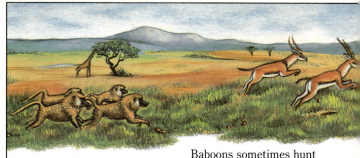

Baboons sometimes hunt young antelope.

In the morning, apes search for food. A menu of their favorites includes bananas, leaves, fruit, buds, seeds... and even insects and small lizards.

Chimpanzees make use of a simple tool. They poke a blade of grass into a termite mound, then eat the insects clinging to the blade when it is pulled out.

A real gourmet, the **orang-utang** travels far to gather leechees, figs and durians, big prickly fruits which he loves. He picks and peels them carefully.

To drink: dewdrops
Most monkeys drink the water from leaves, or drops of dew. Others climb down to ponds or streams. They scoop up water in the palms of their hands, or lick their wet fur. Watch out for crocodiles!

The orang-utang hangs from a branch to drink. Careful: he can't swim!

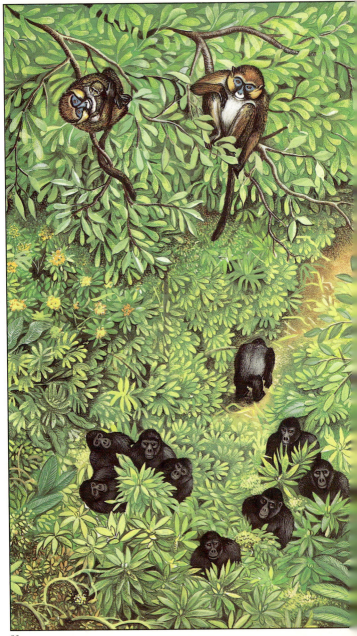

Chimpanzees sleep in a nest of branches covered with leaves.

It's bedtime
Monkeys and apes sleep all night. They also take long naps! Monkeys sleep together in groups for protection. They sleep sitting up in the fork of a tree.

A new nest every night
Some great apes build a platform in the trees, away from their enemies. Only the mother ape sleeps with her young. Adult male gorillas sleep on beds of branches on the ground.

The fork-marked dwarf lemur sleeps in a hollow tree during the day.

At birth, the baby baboon clings to his mother to nurse.

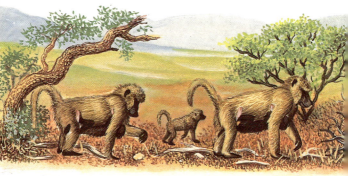

The babies travel everywhere, holding on upside down. Mothers can even hold them with one hand while running.

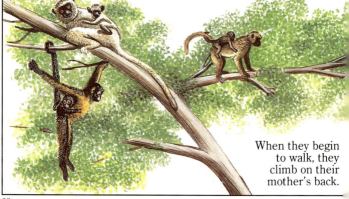

When they begin to walk, they climb on their mother's back.

One baby at a time
Most female monkeys have just one baby at a time. The baby is very small and wrinkly. He is very curious and learns by imitating his mother. When he is afraid, he clings to her.

The baby macaque walks in about a month.

The birth of a baby is a big event for baboons: they all want to touch him! Once a female has a baby, she is respected. The old leader will sit next to her.

The baby gibbon is almost a year old before he climbs by himself.

With his mother, the baby gorilla learns to recognize plants. When he is two, he makes his own nest, but he still stays with his mother. He will live up to fifty years.

The baby gorilla stays with his mother until he is four years old.

The gorilla beats his chest, lets out a terrifying roar and charges to scare off his enemy.

Watch out for leopards!

also eagles and pythons, hunting—
How do monkeys get away? A sentry
sounds the alarm and they scatter.
Baboons bare scary-looking fangs.
They have to watch out for human
hunters, too.

The orang-utang throws branches at his enemy's head.

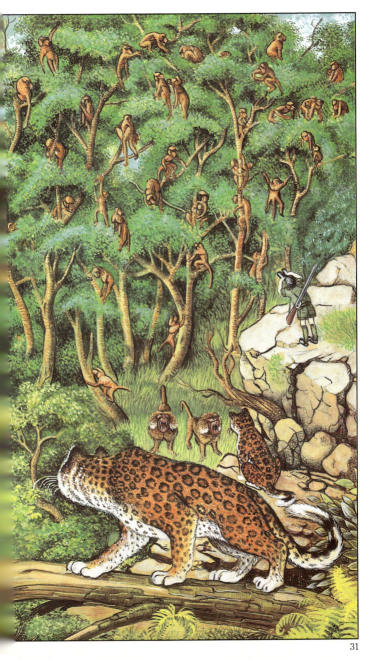

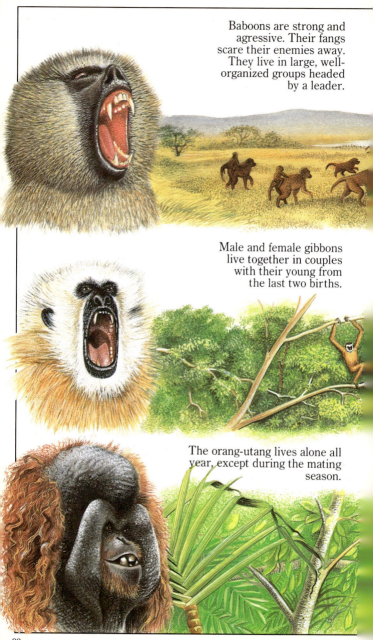

Baboons are strong and agressive. Their fangs scare their enemies away. They live in large, well-organized groups headed by a leader.

Male and female gibbons live together in couples with their young from the last two births.

The orang-utang lives alone all year, except during the mating season.

Lookouts warn the group of approaching danger.

Every morning, they wake the forest with a song like a bird call.

Once the baby is born, only the mother will raise it. The male's puffed-up cheeks make him look tough!

What did man's ancestors look like ten million years ago?

A little like a chimpanzee. The dinosaurs were already extinct by the time early man appeared. Five million years ago, man began to walk erect.

He ate plants and small animals.

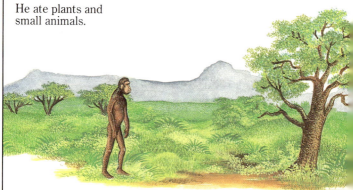

His feet were almost like yours, with all five toes lined up.

Now that he walked on two feet, he could use his hands to throw rocks and defend himself.

Then he invented tools!
He hit rocks together to
give them sharp edges.
He used them to hunt,
chop wood and cut
animal hides.

He sharpened flint, bones and ivory.

Then he raised animals and planted
seeds to grow vegetables. He no
longer had to wander. The first
villages were built 10,000 years ago!

Do you know King Kong?
This famous gorilla never existed except in the movies. He was powerful and frightened many people, but he also wanted to be loved…

Who is the abominable snowman?
This legendary creature
half ape, half man,
is also known as
the **yeti**.
Sometimes, footprints are
found on the snow-covered
slopes of the Himalayas
between India and Tibet.
But they probably belong
to a bear or a
snub-nosed monkey,
a large, furry
mountain monkey.
You may never
see a yeti!

Index

acrobats, 22-23
baboon, 9, 24, 28-32
babies, 28-29, 32-33
biggest, 15
chimpanzee, 6-7, 9, 15, 24, 27
drink, 15, 25
early man, 34
feet, 10, 34
food, 18, 24-25
gibbon, 9, 15, 22-23, 29, 32
gorilla, 9-10, 22, 29-30
great apes, 15, 27

hand, 10, 28, 34
hunters, 30
lemur, 8, 10, 13, 21, 27
mandrill, 10
nocturnal, 10
orang-utang, 9, 15, 25, 32
primate, 10
sleep, 27
smallest, 13, 18
species, 7
strongest, 15
tool, 24, 35